Alphabet
Animals

•

Amphibians
Birds
Reptiles
Endangered
& Mythical
Creatures

Barbra Holt Simpson
with contributions by Beau Stephen Simpson

Barbra Holt Simpson

Printed in USA
November 2014
Designed by Graphic Directions, Inc.
Published by Starboard Main Press
ISBN-13 978-098921704
ISBN-10 0989821706
LCCN 2014935105

Dedicated to
Jay, Steven, Laura & Beau

The great loves of my life.

WRITTEN & ILLUSTRATED BY BARBRA HOLT SIMPSON
WITH CONTRIBUTIONS BY BEAU STEPHEN SIMPSON
BOOK DESIGN BY JAY SIMPSON

Alligator

An Alligator with a reggae beat
crawled from the swamp and walked the street,
looking for a chicken or something good to eat.
Wild birds are NOT his favorite treat.

Bear

A Peanut Butter Bear
left his lair
in the spring
and promptly ate
all the food
that I could bring.
He liked especially
sweet honey,
and his peanut butter
runny,
then climbed up
my
tree
for a swing.

Camel

A Camel for hire
just by the hour,
don't get him upset.
He can really spit.

Camel for you?
One hump or two?
A Camel for hire
just by the hour.

Dragons

Dragons! Dragons!
Dragons are creatures of old.
Hiding! Hiding!
Hiding in caves with their gold.

Dragons breathe fire so they say,
watch where you play,
this may be the day.
Show me the way.

Searching! Searching!
Search for the gold,
if you're really bold.
Dragons! Dragons!

Elephant

A Baby
Elephant
has to learn
to drink
and
dunk
with his
trunk.

He drinks water
through his nose,
holds it tightly
closed,
and sprays
and plays
like a hose!

Fox

The fox is both charming and sly.
Lives a life secluded and shy.
     He sat there scratching, paying no mind,
      when a big fat chicken struts up from behind.

Now he sleeps in his den,
had for breakfast that noisy hen,
     for his dinner, a chicken pot pie.

Quicker
than a blink
of his eye.

Giraffe

Giraffe stretches her neck to the sky
to eat tender leaves up so high.

By the time that she swallows,
    her stomach
    sounds hollow.
    She must have
    a constant
    supply!

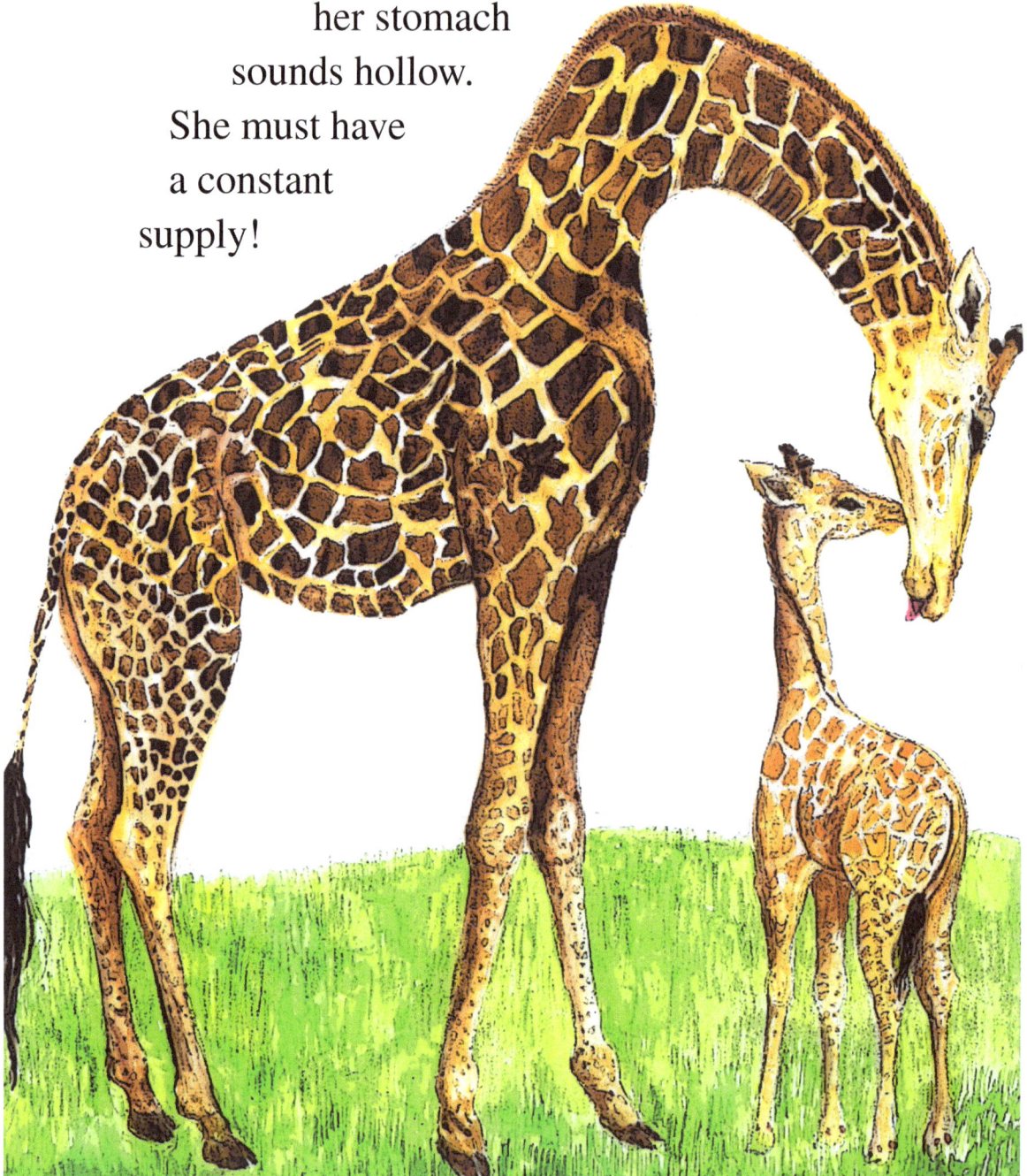

Hippopotamus

Hippopotamus
loves papyrus rush,
agapanthus
and
narcissus lush.
Underwater thus,
he walks effortless.
With jaws so cavernous,
he is not beauteous.

Iguana

Iguanas, lazing in the sun,
warming up
so they can run.

Green Iguanas
run fast through trees
under the leaves.

When they hear
hawk's
warning cries,
as she circles
in the sky,
little ones stay
very still.
Hawks can see
very well.

Jackal

Ding
 Dong
  Bell!
 Jackal's in the well.

 How he got there
 I won't tell.
  Ding, Dong,
  Ding, Dong!
Give the boys a shout!
They will get him out!
 Ding
  Dong
 Ding
  Dong
 Ding
  Dong
   Bell!
 Jackal went
  hunting –
  and fell
  in the well.

Kangaroo

Kangaroo, jump!
Jump, Kangaroo!
Jump, jump, jumping
all around.

Jump, jump, jump!
Jump, Kangaroo!
Jump with both feet
on the ground.

Joey's in the pouch
so he will not fall out.
Jump, jump,
jump!
Jump, Kangaroo!

Lynx

Leopard

Lion

The African Lynx, perched high in the rocks, looks down on the grasslands below. A great Lion's roar can lift all the hairs straight up on my head, and makes the Leopard leap into trees, to be safe in his branch bed.

Monkey

by Beau Simpson, 10 years old

Monkey, monkey sitting in a tree
Sitting on a bee you didn't see!

Screech! Screech!
Screech! Screech!

Swinging wild,
swinging free,
Looking for that bee
you didn't see!

Screech! Screech!
Screech! Screech!

Nanny Goat

Annie's little Nanny Goat
nibbled on her petticoat
while they were waiting in a line.
She thought it tasted mighty fine
until it stuck
in her throat,
She had to cough it up.
Yuck!

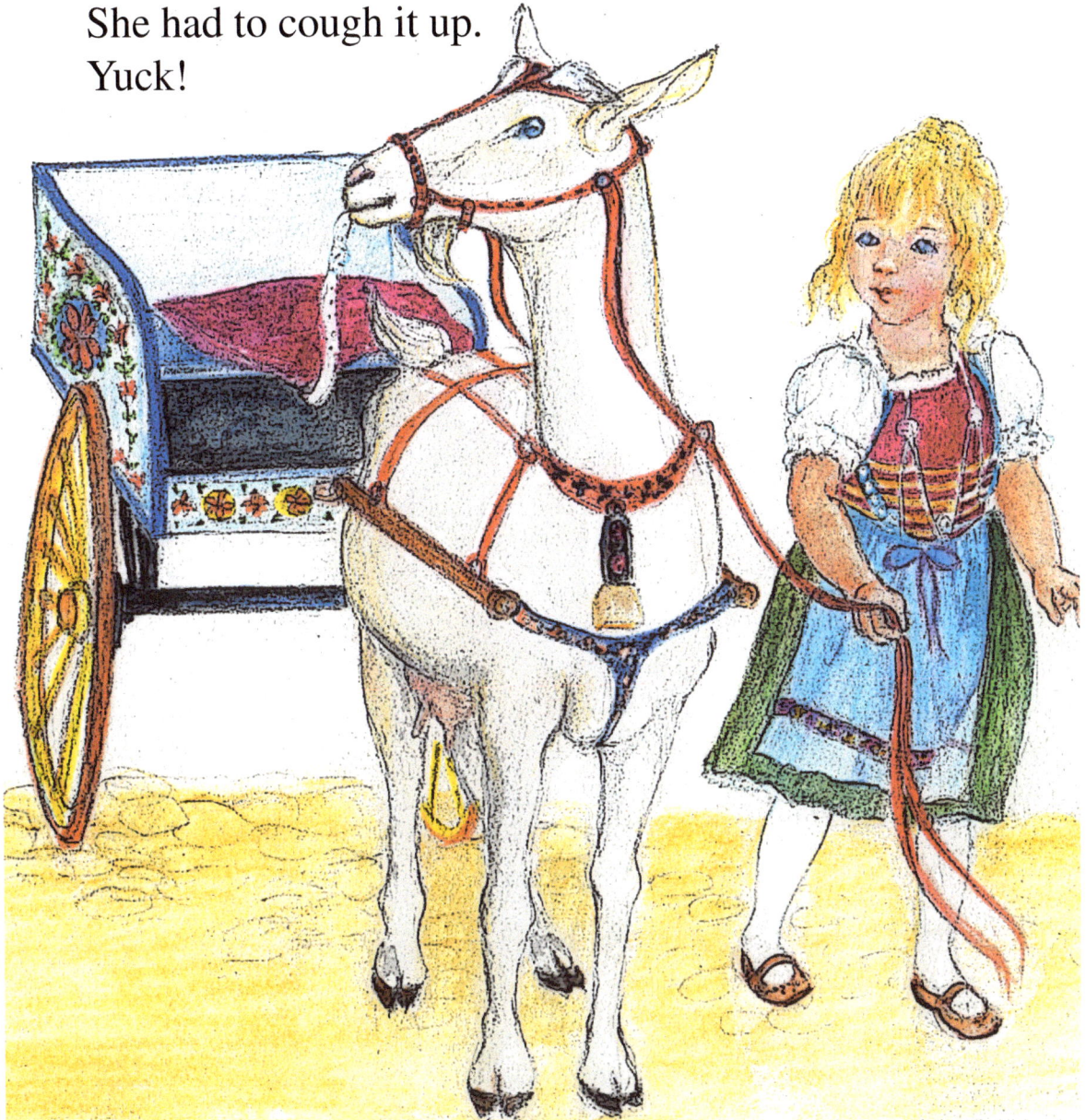

Ostrich

Ostrich is a bird
tall and lanky lean
legs as long as poles
and hides his head
in holes.

(He thinks he
can't be seen.)
His kicks are quick
and mean.

Runs fast
like a horse,
it's true.

And in any race
few could
match his pace.

Pelican

Puffins,
penguins,
pelicans, too!
Peregrine,
pigeons,
Kalamazoo!

Pewee,
phoebe,
picadae sing!
Pintail,
partridge,
peacock king!

Parrots,
parakeets
fill up a tree!
More birds than
I ever did see!

Quetzal

The quetzal of Mexico City,
has feathers that are so pretty
they shimmer a bright golden green,
the most beautiful ever been seen.

One day he was flying by
and caught the emperor's eye,
who saw the long glistening tail
that made other feathers
look pale.

He said,
"I want some
of those, for a cape
that touches
my toes
it matches the
ring in my nose."

He wears it
where ever
he goes.

Rhinoceros

by Beau Simpson, 10 years old

Yo, Rhino!
Rhinoceros rap
is the coolest thing,
it just makes me feel
like I want to swing.
God makes them
and he shakes them
and he takes them out,
right next door
to the camel's house.

Salamanders

Salamanders, slick and slimy.
Salamanders slithery, slippery,
    shunning the sun in caves,
    sleeping through the days.

Salamanders slinky, silly,
swim in streams and rivers rilly.
    Some are black or white,
    others spotted bright,

swimming silently
in dark of night.

Turtles

Turtles in the ocean blue
can end up in somebody's stew.

The eggs are buried on the beach
and hatchlings scamper out of reach.

We can help them swim free
from nets in the sea.

Let's help them at birth
and help Mother Earth.

Unicorn

A mythical creature born with one horn tamed by a girl who named him, 'Unicorn.'

Vampire Bat

A Vampire Bat
uses sonar to see.
His eyes aren't sharp,
but they don't
need to be.
Large ears
locate echoes
to tell this from that.
He sleeps through the day,
hunts at night far away
for horses, cows or men.
He pierces the skin,
sinks sharp teeth in,
and sucks the blood away.
  Vanessa never plays
  in the park
  after dark.

Wolves

White Wolves howl in the arctic snow
where raging white winds blow.
In this icy land of the midnight sun
night and day are as one.
On soft, starry nights
or moonlight bright,
Wolves lonely cries,
sing through the night.

Xenophus

African frogs
swimming in bogs
or sitting on logs.
Ribbit. Ribbit.

Croaking in chorus
symphonious hum-m-m.
Singing in chorus
harmonious, hum-m-m.

Yak

In windswept
highlands of Tibet,
lives a girl who milks a Nak,
makes butter and cheese
for a snack,
leads her black Yak
with a backpack
from Ladakh to Tienshan
in a caravan.

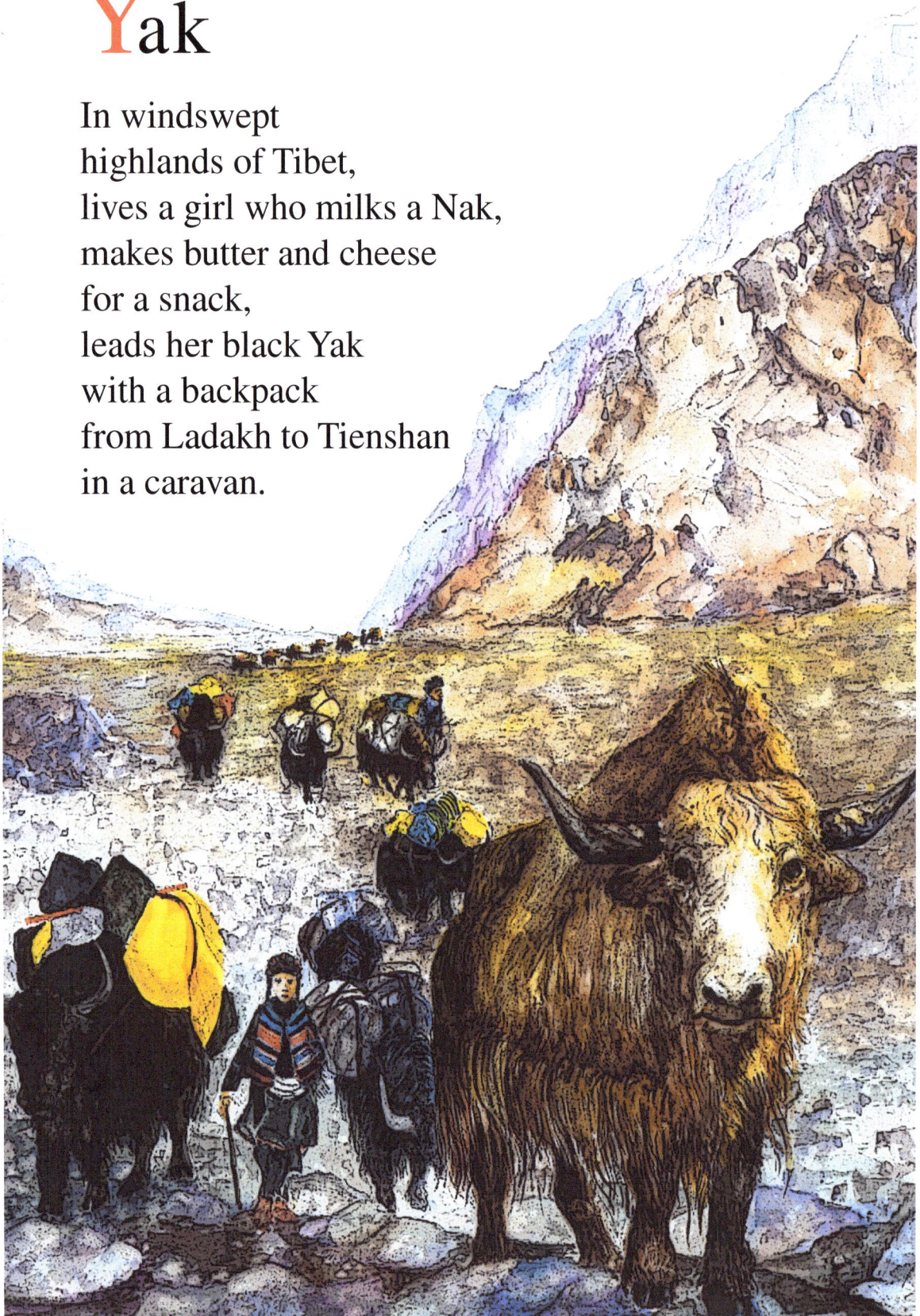

Zebra

Zacharia and Zedidiah
met a Zebra at the zoo,
who gave them quite a friendly look
because they wore stripes, too.

Zebras striped black and white,
like shadows of grass in the wind,
they eat and run in bright daylight,
to escape from lions and men.

Where are the Cape Zebras left to run?
This may be the only one!

THE END

Alphabet Animals:
Amphibians, Birds, Reptiles, Endangered and Mythical Creatures

A book of Poems for Children
by Barbra Holt Simpson.

The poems are both fun and educational. Colorful illustrations highlight wildlife in the real world and mythical creatures.

Consciousness of our natural world begins early in our children's lives. Natural habitats are being destroyed, leaving fewer places of safety. Today, only four white rhinocerous remain, separated in zoos, no longer in their own environment. With education, awareness, and action we can save our precious heritage for future generations.

Mr. Sly Fox
loves chickens.

What happens when a
chicken gets too close?

What do you think?

Barbra Holt Simpson

The author lives with her husband and daughter in California.
She began writing poetry for her first child, Steven.
After her special needs daughter, Laura, was born,
Barbra illustrated and bound individual books
for her. Barbra has a Master of Fine Arts
degree in drawing and painting.

Alphabet Animals:
Amphibians, Birds, Reptiles, Endangered and Mythical Creatures
a poetry book written for her grandson,
Beau,

SNOWY OWL
A Bedtime Story

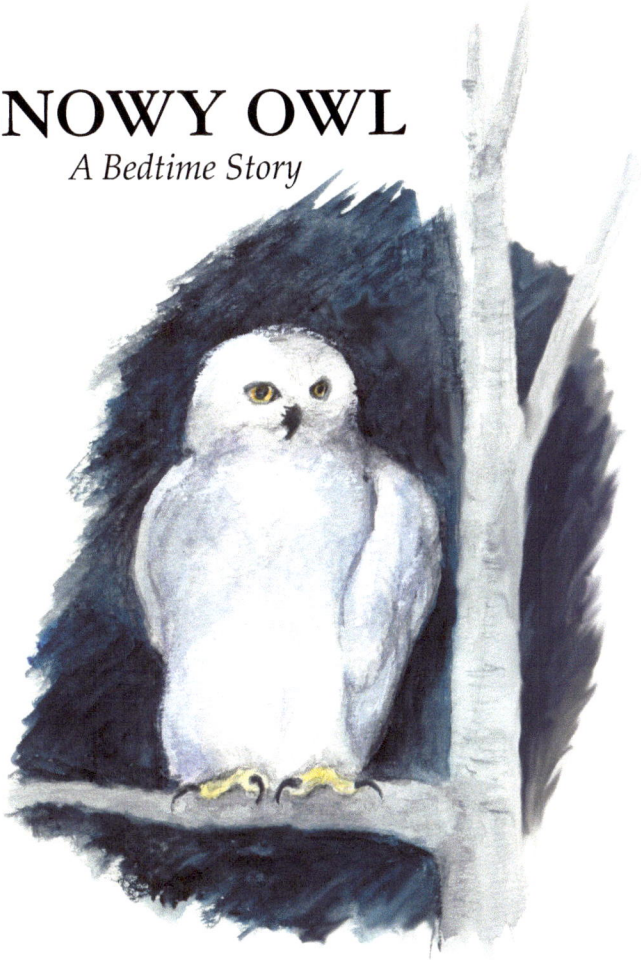

by Barbra Holt Simpson

A Little Owl sleeps
safe beneath his mother's wing.

What happens when they
are forced to leave
their mountain home?

How will they find a
new place to live?

Barbra Simpson's new book for children
SNOWY OWL
will be available from amazon.com.

This picture book bedtime story tells of
a little owl's peaceful life with his mother,
interrupted by a forest fire that changes
their lives forever.

barbraholtsimpson.com
barbra_holt_simpson@aol.

www.ingramcontent.com/pod-product-compliance
Lightning Source LLC
Chambersburg PA
CBHW060835270326
41933CB00002B/99